591
Car

D1408728

ANIMALS ON THE MOVE

Regular 1990-91 Garrett 6/4/90 $13.95

Hubbard Elem. School Library
Culloden Road
Forsyth, GA 31029

U.S. text © 1989 by Garrett Educational Corporation
First published in the United States in 1989 by
Garrett Educational Corporation, 130 East 13th Street,
Ada, OK 74820

Original edition published in England under the title of:

FINDING OUT ABOUT
ANIMALS ON THE MOVE

Copyright © 1987 Ilex Publishers Limited

All rights reserved. No part of this publication may be
reproduced, stored in a retrieval system, or transmitted
in any form or by any means, electronic, mechanical,
photocopying, recording or otherwise, without the
permission of the publisher and the copyright holder.

Manufactured in the United States of America

Library of Congress Cataloging in Publication Data

Carwardine, Mark.
    Animals on the move / written by Mark Carwardine; illustrated by
John Francis.
        p. cm. — (Looking at how animals live)
    "An Ilex book."
    Summary: Describes the appearance, behavior, and locomotion of a
variety of animals, including the swift, Arctic tern, mudskipper,
kangaroo, and red-billed quelea.
    1. Animals—Juvenile literature.   2. Animal locomotion—Juvenile
literature.   [1. Animals.   2. Animal locomotion.]   I. Francis,
John, 1942-   ill.   II. Title.   III. Series: Carwardine, Mark.
Looking at how animals live.
QL49.C36   1989
591—dc20   89-32809
    ISBN 0-944483-27-5   CIP
                                                                AC

LOOKING AT HOW ANIMALS LIVE

ANIMALS ON THE MOVE

Written by Mark Carwardine
Illustrated by John Francis

An Ilex Book

GARRETT EDUCATIONAL CORPORATION

CONTENTS

Swift

Swifts spend most of their lives in the air. They fly non-stop from the moment they leave their nests to the day they begin building nests of their own.

By the time they land for the first time, they have been flying for up to three years and have travelled over three hundred thousand miles.

Unlike many birds, swifts find it very difficult to perch and almost impossible to walk. However, since they like to nest on large buildings — even in city centers — they have very strong feet for grasping onto brick walls.

Swifts sleep and eat in the air. Their long wings help them to glide and fly, wheeling and turning for hours on end. Sometimes they fly hundreds of miles in a single day while feeding, catching insects with their enormous beaks. They return to feed their chicks with mouthfuls of food about every half an hour or so. A single mouthful may contain over a thousand tiny insects.

Swifts are among the fastest-flying birds in the world. The white-throated spinetail swift of Asia is the overall record-holder, able to reach speeds of over one hundred miles an hour.

Arctic tern

In its lifetime, an arctic tern flies far enough to travel to the moon and back. Every year it migrates from one end of the world to the other — often between the Arctic and the Antarctic — and back again. As a result, it stays in the air for no less than eight months out of every twelve.

Arctic terns are very graceful and agile birds. They usually live near the sea, where they feed on fish, squid and other small animals. Flying low over the water, they carefully search for their food before hovering a few feet above the surface and then diving in headfirst for the catch.

Arctic terns can live for up to thirty years. They pair for life, the same females and males always breeding together, and they usually nest in busy and noisy colonies. There is safety in numbers, and they often gang up on enemies such as skuas to chase them away. They even dive-bomb people, and will hit hard with their beaks and draw blood if the intruders do not go away.

When the nesting season is over, the male and female terns split up before flying south. They do not see one another again for nearly a year, until it is time to meet in the same colony the next season.

Gray whale

Twice a year gray whales swim along the entire length of the west coast of North America. The return trip, between the Arctic Ocean or Alaska and Mexico, is more than twelve thousand miles.

They spend the summer months feeding in the cold waters of the north. Plowing along the seabed with their mouths, they eat small fish, seaweed, shellfish and shrimps by filtering them out of the sand and dirt. In late autumn they stop feeding and begin to move south. Staying very close to the shore, they swim about a hundred and fifty miles every day. Two months later they arrive in Baja California, Mexico, where they breed before returning north again the following spring.

The gray whale is about fifty feet long and can weigh as much as thirty-eight tons. Its tongue alone weighs nearly one and a half tons. Like all whales, it has to come to the surface to breathe. Its spout, which is caused by water spraying into the air as it breathes out through its blowhole, is thirteen feet high and can be heard from nearly a mile away.

Gray whales are very popular animals. Even though they were once hunted almost to extinction, they seem to like people and will even swim up to small boats to have their heads stroked.

11

Sidewinder

The sidewinder is a strange snake that travels sideways. It seems to fly along the ground, as if on a magic carpet, and can travel at more than two miles per hour.

The sidewinder lives in the deserts of western North America. It can slide along like other snakes but "sidewinding," as its special way of moving is called, is the best way of travelling across loose sand.

Although it is a kind of rattlesnake and often seen during the daytime, the sidewinder is not particularly dangerous. It comes out at night to hunt for smaller snakes and lizards, but spends many hours resting quietly on the sand or just below the surface. Only its eyes — which are protected by small horns on the top of its head — stick out like little periscopes.

Sidewinders give birth to up to fifteen young snakes in the late autumn. Each of the babies is about ten inches long, which is roughly one third the length of their parents. They quickly become expert sidewinders and soon join the adults in their strange travels across the desert.

Gecko

The gecko is the noisiest lizard in the world. It spends a great deal of its time chirping, squeaking, barking and clicking to other geckos nearby. But it is best known for being able to walk on walls and upside down on ceilings.

Often found inside houses and other buildings, geckos are very common animals in many parts of the world. They do not have special suction pads on their feet — as many people believe — but use hairs underneath their toes as miniature hooks. These hooks look like the bristles of a brush and catch onto the tiniest bumps and dips on any surface. They even enable the geckos to run up and down windowpanes and mirrors.

Occasionally, geckos do make mistakes and fall off — especially when they are fighting — but then they simply run back to the nearest wall and dash up to the ceiling again, as if nothing had happened.

To help them see in the dark, geckos have enormous eyes which they lick to keep clean. Completely harmless creatures, they are very popular because they eat spiders, beetles, cockroaches and many other bugs.

Peregrine

The peregrine falcon is probably the fastest-moving animal in the world. When hunting it is capable of more incredible feats of speed and skill in the air than almost anything else that flies.

The peregrine feeds on other birds. Pigeons and grouse are its favorite prey, but it will catch almost anything from a starling to a goose. It has excellent eyesight and, when just a mere speck high up in the sky, is able to spot a likely bird flying a long way below.

Folding back its wings, it begins to drop like a stone towards its quarry. Incredible speeds of one hundred twenty-five miles an hour or more are often reached during these dives.

The bird below has to be very quick — and lucky — to escape. On most occasions it is killed outright with a single blow from the peregrine's claws, instantly breaking the prey's neck or back.

Peregrines prefer to live around cliffs, both inland and along the coast, but can also be seen over wetlands and estuaries. Their nests, known as eyries, are usually placed on bare rock ledges.

The eggs take a month to hatch, and the young peregrine chicks are ready to fly from their clifftop homes after about six weeks.

Hubbard Elem. School Library

Koala

Koalas look just like bears. But they are actually related to kangaroos, and female koalas even have pouches on their bellies to prove it.

They live in gum trees in southeastern Australia. Once they were very common animals, but many have been killed over the years for food and for their thick, warm fur. Today, however, koalas are carefully protected and their numbers are slowly increasing.

Koalas are excellent climbers, able to grasp tree trunks and branches firmly with their fingers and toes, using their sharp claws to dig into the bark. But koalas find it very difficult to move on the ground. They rarely leave the safety of their treetop homes but, when they have to, they shuffle along slowly and climb another trunk as soon as they can.

18

Koalas spend most of their time sleeping and dozing. They are active for only a few hours during the middle of the night, when they eat as many leaves and as much bark as they possibly can before going back to sleep.

A baby koala is about the size of a grape when it is first born. So it climbs into the safety of its mother's pouch while it grows bigger. After about six months, it ventures out to travel around on her back until it is about a year old and can look after itself.

Chamois

The chamois is a daring, agile and graceful animal. It is famous for its incredible sense of balance and breathtaking leaps. About the size of a goat, it can easily jump twelve feet high and nearly twenty feet forward.

Chamois are found in the dangerous mountainous country of central and southern Europe. They live mainly in the Pyrenees, the Alps and the Apennines. More sure-footed and nimble than any mountaineer could ever hope to be, there are very few places which they cannot reach by climbing or jumping.

Young chamois learn their mountaineering skills very quickly. After a few practice jumps on and off their mothers' backs, they happily follow the rest of the herd wherever it goes. When danger approaches, members of the herd stamp their feet and whistle.

They all flee to some inaccessible spot on the mountain — and the young have to be able to keep up.

Chamois move up and
down the mountain with the
seasons, to avoid heavy snow
as much as possible. In the
summer, they eat herbs and
flowers, but change to
lichens, mosses and young
pine shoots as they move
downhill in the winter.

21

Tawny owl

The tawny owl has special feathers to help it fly in complete silence. It can glide down to catch a mouse, shrew or vole without making the slightest sound.

Tawny owls are very familiar birds as they are found in many towns and cities over much of Europe and Asia. Although they come out at night, their well-known hooting always gives their presence away. They have large eyes, to help them see in the dark, and sensitive ears for listening to the night-time rustlings of their prey.

They can occasionally be seen in the daytime as well. Hunched up asleep in a tree, they are often mobbed by smaller birds such as robins, chaffinches and thrushes. These birds make such a noise that they attract attention to the unfortunate owls.

Tawny owls begin nesting in early March. They lay up to five eggs on leaves and moss in the bottom of a hole in a tree. One month later, the eggs hatch and the young owls — called owlets — are fed by their parents for about five weeks. Once they have left the nesting hole, they remain together as a family for another three months, before the young leave home to fend for themselves.

Mudskipper

The mudskipper is a fish which behaves more like a newt. It spends some of its time in the water with other fish but prefers to be out on the land. Sometimes it even climbs small trees.

Mudskippers live in the mangrove swamps and muddy estuaries of the tropics. They are so fond of the land that some of them even build mud walls around themselves, several feet long, to stop other mudskippers from entering their private territories.

They fight and court one another out of the water and find their food — which includes insects, tiny worms, shellfish and small plants — in the mud well away from the water's edge.

But they still breathe through gills, like other fish. Instead of always staying underwater, though, they simply return to collect mouthfuls of water at regular intervals. They can also breathe through their skin.

Mudskippers are able to move about on land in two different ways. To move quickly, in a series of little jumps, they curl their tails to the side and flick themselves forward. But if they want to move more slowly, they haul themselves along using their front fins as crutches.

25

Condor

The condor can survive for several weeks without eating. But when it finds food — usually a dead animal — it often eats so much that it cannot take off. The only solution is to walk up a nearby hill and jump into the air.

Like other members of the vulture family, the condor is an ugly bird on the ground.

But in the air it is beautiful and graceful, able to soar effortlessly for hours on end without needing to flap its wings. With a wingspan of nearly ten feet, it is one of the largest flying birds in the world. One of its extinct relatives was even bigger, measuring twice as much from wingtip to wingtip.

There are two different kinds of condor. One lives in the Andes of South America and the other is found in a small part of California. They are both uncommon birds, and the Californian condor is now so rare that only a few dozen are left in the wild. It may soon become extinct.

Condors nest in cliff caves and inside hollow trees. They breed only once every two years, laying just one egg at a time. The newly hatched chick is carefully looked after by its parents for more than a year. It does not breed itself until it is at least seven years old.

Hummingbird

Hummingbirds in flight beat their wings so fast that they are only visible as a blur. They flap up and down almost eighty times every second and enable the birds to hover in midair.

There are over three hundred different kinds of hummingbirds, found in North, Central and South America. They are all beautifully colored birds, in glittering greens, blues, purples, reds and yellows.

Most hummingbirds feed on small insects and nectar. They hover in front of a flower and reach inside with their long bills to drink. The bill of one hummingbird is more than four inches long.

Because they use up a great deal of energy in flight, hummingbirds need a tremendous amount of food. So most hummingbirds eat and drink over half their body weight every day.

Hummingbirds build small nests on the top of twigs or tiny branches, often tying them on safely with cobwebs. They lay two very tiny eggs which hatch after a few weeks. The female does all the work — building the nest, sitting on the eggs and feeding the young — by herself.

She spends hours every
day collecting nectar and
insects and injecting them into
the nestlings' throats through
her bill. But the male takes no
interest at all. He has no idea
where the nest is hidden —
and will probably never see
the baby birds.

29

Kangaroo

Some kangaroos are able to cover more than twenty-five feet in a single hop. Using their long hind legs to jump and their enormous tails to keep balance in midair, they can sometimes reach speeds of over thirty miles per hour.

Kangaroos are found in Australia and New Guinea. They live in open plains, woodlands and forests and rocky areas. Some of the smaller kinds even live in trees.

They range in size from the musky rat kangaroo, which is about as small as a rat, to the red and gray kangaroos, which are taller than a man. Most kinds feed on grass and other plants, though some also eat small animals such as insects and worms.

When kangaroos are feeding, they move along quite slowly, often using their tails as stools to sit on.

Kangaroos usually have one tiny baby, called a joey. As soon as it is born, the joey crawls into the safety of its mother's pouch. It stays there for several months, growing and developing, before venturing into the outside world. At first it is very nervous and, if danger threatens, will run back to its mother and dive into her pouch headfirst.

Flying fox

In many parts of the tropical and subtropical regions of the world, hundreds or thousands of foxlike animals can be seen hanging upside down — by their feet — from the treetops. Their coats are reddish-brown, and they have foxy faces, with large eyes and small ears.

Known as flying "foxes," these strange creatures are actually bats.

With wingspans of over six feet, the flying foxes, or fruit bats as they are sometimes called, are the largest bats in the world. They live mainly in forests and swamps, from Africa to east Asia and Australasia.

Roosting in the trees all day, they are very noisy animals, always squabbling or calling to one another. They rarely stay still for long, preferring to stretch a wing or fan themselves to keep cool, rather than resting quietly.

As soon as dusk begins to fall, the bats begin to get noisier and even more fidgety than earlier in the day. Before dark they can wait no longer and are on their way to the best feeding sites. These are sometimes as far as forty-five miles away and may involve a flight of several hours. The bats leave their colonies in small parties. One by one they let their feet go and drop into the air, until their huge wings stop the fall and take them steadily on their way. They spend the night feeding on fruit and on the pollen and nectar of flowers before returning home in time for sunrise.

Wildebeest

Every year, at the beginning of the dry season, enormous herds of wildebeest patiently follow one another in single file across the plains of East and southern Africa. They may travel over six hundred miles before they reach water and fresh pasture.

In the Serengeti, in Tanzania, there are often more than a million wildebeest, joined by zebras, gazelles and other animals, swimming across rivers and winding their way over the plains like a long, slow-moving train.

As soon as the dry season is over and the rains change the parched grasslands back to green pasture, the animals make their return journey home.

Over three feet tall at the shoulder, the wildebeest, or gnu, spends much of its time eating grass. A very weird-looking animal, it even acts strangely, often prancing about, digging its horns into the earth, pawing the ground and thrashing its tail.

The males try to attract females by calling to them with their loud, deep grunts. But the grunts sound more like croaking frogs and very often are ignored. So they give chase and try to keep the females within their territories in order to mate.

Baby wildebeest are able to stand within minutes after being born, and only need a few days' practice before they can run fast enough to keep up with the rest of the herd.

Pine marten

At first sight, the pine marten looks more like a giant squirrel. But it actually belongs to an entirely different family of animals which includes otters, badgers and ferrets.

About the size of a large cat, with a rich chocolate brown coat and a long, bushy tail, it is a strikingly beautiful animal.

Pine martens are found in many parts of Europe and as far east as Asia. Very agile animals, they prefer to live in woodlands, where they race around in the trees squirrel-fashion. They are able to fall sixty-five feet from a branch and land on the ground on all fours, completely unharmed, and can also run very fast over short distances.

Pine martens are active both at night and during the day. They feed on many different animals, including voles and other rodents, small birds, beetles, caterpillars, birds' eggs, berries and, in some areas, even red squirrels.

Their nests are hidden in rocky crevices, holes in river banks, abandoned squirrel dreys or old birds' nests. Three young are born, usually in March or April, and they emerge from the den for the first time after about two months. It isn't until early winter, however, that they are completely independent and able to look after themselves.

Spiny anteater

When they are frightened, spiny anteaters can burrow into the ground so fast that it looks as if they are sinking. But if the ground is too hard to dig, they have other methods of escape or defense. They curl up into a spiky ball, or they dive into a nearby hiding place with only the spines on their backs still visible.

Spiny anteaters, or echidnas, are very unusual mammals because they lay eggs. The female lays a single leathery egg and carries it in her pouch for about ten days. When it hatches, the baby echidna is tiny, blind and hairless.

At first no bigger than a grape, it grows very rapidly and has to leave the safety of its mother's pouch as soon as the sharp spines begin to appear.

Spiny anteaters live in the mountains, forest, plains and valleys of Australia and New Guinea. Over three feet long, they live alone for most of the year, wandering around at dusk or dawn in search of food. They hate the rain and will shelter for days on end until it stops and they can, at last, continue sniffing around for insects and earthworms. Those that eat insects tear open logs and underground nests, sticking their tongues — which are up to seven inches long — in and out to pick up the ants and termites. Anteaters that eat mostly earthworms hook them on a row of tiny spines on their tongues and haul them in for chewing.

Frog

The goliath frog from West Africa is able to jump more than nine feet along the ground. One of its smaller relatives, a tree frog, can leap out of a tree and glide fifty feet or more through the air, using its webbed feet as small parachutes.

These and many other frogs throughout the world are famous for their leaping abilities. They leap to get from one place to another, or to escape from their enemies. Indeed, they seem to disappear so quickly that they are almost impossible to catch.

Some kinds, however, have rather different forms of defense. There are those so perfectly camouflaged that, when they are crouching on the ground, they become almost invisible against their leafy backgrounds.

In Central and South America, other frogs produce special poisons that can kill a bird or monkey within seconds. They are the most attractive frogs of all, but their bright colors tell larger animals that they are poisonous — and warn them to stay away.

Frogs, and their close relatives the toads, are found almost anywhere there is fresh water or moisture, from tropical jungles to parts of the Arctic. There are more than two thousand six hundred different kinds altogether, most easily distinguished by their skins. Those with smooth skins are called frogs; those with drier, warty skins are called toads.

Flying fish

In many tropical oceans of the world there lives a fish that really can fly. It shoots out of the water and into the air at nearly twenty miles an hour. Then it glides for nearly one-third of a mile before falling back into the sea. Sometimes the flying fish misjudges its flight and lands on the deck of a ship by mistake.

The fins of flying fish have grown much bigger than in most other fish, to form their "wings." They do not flap but are used more like the wings of a hang-glider, to soar through the air. Sometimes the fish are able to catch good air currents and can rise fifteen feet or more above the surface of the sea.

When a flying fish leaps into the air it is usually being chased. By flying out of the water it has a better chance of escaping. It takes off by thrashing its tail to help it burst through the surface as quickly as possible.

But some predators continue to chase the fish and try to grab them as their flights come to an end and they fall back into the water. In these cases, they let their tails dip under the surface and thrash away once again to launch into another flight. Even then, they are not assured of safety. They also have to keep an eye open for seabirds, which sometimes catch and eat flying fish in midair.

Red-billed quelea

The red-billed quelea is the most common bird in the world. There are more than ten billion of them living south of the Sahara Desert in Africa. They sometimes fly in flocks of hundreds of thousands, so densely packed that they blacken the sky. From a distance, a quelea flock looks more like a smoke cloud and can easily be heard, as the birds make a lot of noise constantly chattering to one another.

When the queleas stop flying and settle in the trees, their sheer weight is often enough to break off branches.

Although rather sparrow-like, red-billed queleas belong to a group of birds known as the weavers. They nest in enormous colonies, in carefully woven grass ball nests. Sometimes there are more than five hundred nests in a single tree. They usually breed between November and April — laying up to four eggs, which hatch after about two weeks.

Unfortunately, many of the young queleas fall out of their nests and are eaten by other animals. But the parents continue bringing insects to feed the survivors until they are old enough to fend for themselves.

The adult birds eat mostly seeds and grain, which they find on the ground by jumping backwards with both feet to scrape away the earth.

Other books in this series

ANIMALS IN THE COLD
MONKEYS AND APES
NIBBLERS AND GNAWERS
NIGHT ANIMALS
WATER ANIMALS